LIFE'S LITTLE
INSTRUCTION BOOK

H. Jackson Brown, Jr.

Thorsons
An Imprint of HarperCollins*Publishers*

Thorsons
An Imprint of HarperCollins*Publishers*
77-85 Fulham Palace Road,
Hammersmith, London W6 8JB

Published by Thorsons 1991
First published in the USA by Rutledge Hill Press, Inc.,
513 Third Avenue South, Nashville, Tennessee 37210, 1991
10

© H. Jackson Brown, Jr. 1991

H. Jackson Brown, Jr. asserts the moral right to
be identified as the author of this work

Cover artwork by Jackie Campbell

A catalogue record for this book
is available from the British Library

ISBN 0 7225 2828 0

Printed in Great Britain by
HarperCollinsManufacturing, Glasgow

INTRODUCTION

This book began as a gift to my son, Adam. As he packed his stereo, typewriter, blue blazer, and other necessities for his new life as a college fresher, I retreated to the family room to jot down a few observations and words of counsel I thought he might find useful.

I read years ago that it was not the responsibility of parents to pave the road for their children, but to provide a road map. That's how I hoped he would use these mind and heart reflections.

I started writing, and what I thought would take a few hours took several days. I gathered my collection of handwritten notes, typed them up, and put them in a file. I walked to the garage and slid it under the front seat of the car.

A few days later his mother and I helped him move into his new digs. When he was all settled in, I asked him to come with me to the car park. It was time for the presentation. I reached under the car seat and, with words to the effect that this was what I knew about living a happy and rewarding life, handed him the bound pages. He hugged me and shook my hand. It was a very special moment.

Well, somehow those typewritten pages became the little book you're now holding. You may not agree with all the entries, and from your own life experience I'm sure you could add hundreds more. Obviously, some are more important than others, but all have added a degree of joy, meaning, and efficiency to my life.

A few days after I had given Adam his copy, he called me from college. 'Dad' he said 'I've been reading the instruction book and I think it's one of the best gifts I've ever received. I'm going to add to it and someday give it to my son.'

Every once in a while life hands you a moment so precious, so overwhelming you almost glow. I know. I just experienced one.

For Adam, my son
and in many ways my teacher.

Son, how can I help you see?
May I give you my shoulders to stand on?
Now you see farther than me.
Now you see for both of us.
Won't you tell me what you see?

1 ♦ Compliment three people every day.

2 ♦ Have a dog.

3 ♦ Watch a sunrise at least once a year.

4 ♦ Remember other people's birthdays.

5 ♦ Overtip breakfast waitresses.

6 ◆ Have a firm handshake.

7 ◆ Look people in the eye.

8 ◆ Say 'thank you' a lot.

9 ◆ Say 'please' a lot.

10 ◆ Learn to play a musical instrument.

11 ♦ Sing in the shower.

12 ♦ Use the good silver.

13 ♦ Learn to make great chilli.

14 ♦ Plant flowers every spring.

15 ♦ Own a great stereo system.

16 ♦ Be the first to say 'Hello'.

17 ♦ Live beneath your means.

18 ♦ Drive inexpensive cars, but own the best house you can afford.

19 ♦ Buy great books even if you never read them.

20 ◆ Be forgiving of yourself and others.

21 ◆ Learn three clean jokes.

22 ◆ Wear polished shoes.

23 ◆ Floss your teeth.

24 ◆ Drink champagne for no reason at all.

25 ◆ Ask for a raise when you feel you've earned it.

26 ◆ If in a fight, hit first and hit hard.

27 ◆ Return all things you borrow.

28 ◆ Teach some kind of class.

29 ◆ Be a student in some kind of class.

30 ♦ Never buy a house without a fireplace.

31 ♦ Buy whatever kids are selling on card tables in their front gardens.

32 ♦ Once in your life own a convertible.

33 ♦ Treat everyone you meet like you want to be treated.

34 ◆ Learn to identify the music of Chopin, Mozart and Beethoven.

35 ◆ Plant a tree on your birthday.

36 ◆ Donate two pints of blood every year.

37 ◆ Make new friends but cherish the old ones too.

38 ◆ Keep secrets.

39 ◆ Take lots of snapshots.

40 ◆ Never refuse homemade biscuits.

41 ◆ Don't postpone joy.

42 ◆ Write 'thank you' notes promptly.

43 ◆ Never give up
on anybody.
Miracles happen
every day.

44 ◆ Show respect for teachers.

45 ◆ Show respect for police officers and firefighters.

46 ◆ Show respect for military personnel.

47 ◆ Don't waste time learning the 'tricks of the trade'. Instead, learn the trade.

48 ◆ Keep a tight rein on your temper.

49 ◆ Buy vegetables from farmers who advertise with hand-lettered signs.

50 ◆ Put the cap back on the toothpaste.

51 ◆ Take out the rubbish without having to be told.

52 ◆ Avoid over-exposure to the sun.

53 ◆ Vote.

54 ◆ Surprise loved ones with little unexpected gifts.

55 ◆ Stop blaming others. Take responsibility for every area of your life.

56 ◆ Never mention being on a diet.

57 ◆ Make the best of bad situations.

58 ◆ Always accept an outstretched hand.

59 ◆ Live so that when your children think of fairness, caring and integrity, they think of you.

60 ◆ Admit your mistakes.

61 ◆ Ask someone to pick up your mail and daily paper when you're out of town. Those are the first two things potential burglars look for.

62 ◆ Use your wit to amuse, not to abuse.

63 ◆ Remember that all news is biased.

64 ◆ Take a photography course.

65 ◆ Let people pull in front of you when you're stopped in traffic.

66 ◆ Support a school orchestra or band.

67 ◆ Demand excellence and be willing to pay for it.

68 ◆ Be brave. Even if you're
not, pretend to be.
No one can tell
the difference.

69 ◆ Whistle.

70 ◆ Hug children after you discipline them.

71 ◆ Learn to make something beautiful with your hands.

72 ◆ Give to charity all the clothes you haven't worn for three years.

73 ◆ Never forget your anniversary.

74 ◆ Eat prunes.

75 ◆ Ride a bike.

76 ◆ Choose a charity in your community
and support it generously with your
time and money.

77 ◆ Don't take good health for granted.

78 ◆ When someone wants to hire you, even if it's for a job you have little interest in, talk to them. Never close the door on an opportunity until you've had a chance to hear the offer in person.

79 ◆ Don't mess with drugs, and don't associate with those who do.

80 ◆ Slow dance.

81 ◆ Avoid sarcastic remarks.

82 ◆ Steer clear of restaurants with strolling musicians.

83 ◆ In business and in family relationships, remember that the most important thing is trust.

84 ♦ Forget the Joneses.

85 ♦ Never encourage anyone to become a lawyer.

86 ♦ Don't smoke.

87 ♦ Attach a small wreath to your car grille at Christmas time.

88 ♦ Even if you are financially well off, have your children earn and pay for their car insurance.

89 ♦ Recycle old newspapers, bottles and cans.

90 ♦ Refill ice cube trays.

91 ♦ Don't let anyone ever see you tipsy.

92 ◆ Never invest more in the stock market than you can afford to lose.

93 ◆ Choose your life's mate carefully. From this one decision will come 90 per cent of all your happiness or misery.

94 ◆ Make it a habit to do nice things for people who'll never find out.

95 ◆ Attend school reunions.

96 ◆ Lend only those books you never care to see again.

97 ◆ Always have something beautiful in sight, even if it's just a daisy in a glass.

98 ◆ Learn how to type.

99 ♦ Think big thoughts,
but relish small pleasures.

100 ◆ Don't do nothing because you feel you can only do a little. Do what you can.

101 ◆ Learn how to read a financial report.

102 ◆ Tell your kids often how terrific they are and that you trust them.

103 ◆ Use credit cards only for convenience, never for credit.

104 ◆ Take a brisk 30-minute walk every day.

105 ◆ Treat yourself to a massage on your birthday.

106 ◆ Never cheat.

107 ◆ Smile a lot. It costs nothing and is beyond price.

108 ♦ When dining with clients or business associates, never order more than one cocktail or one glass of wine. If no one else is drinking, don't drink at all.

109 ♦ Know how to drive a car.

110 ♦ Spread crunchy peanut butter on ginger biscuits for the perfect late-night snack.

111 ◆ Never use profanity.

112 ◆ Never argue with police officers, and address them as 'Officer'.

113 ◆ Learn to identify local wildflowers, birds and trees.

114 ◆ Keep fire extinguishers in your kitchen and car.

115 ◆ Give yourself a year and read the bible cover to cover.

116 ◆ Consider writing a living will.

117 ◆ Install dead bolt locks on all outside doors.

118 ◆ Don't buy expensive wine. luggage or watches.

119 ◆ Put a lot of little marshmallows in your hot chocolate.

120 ◆ Learn mouth-to-mouth resuscitation.

121 ◆ Resist the temptation to buy a boat.

122 ◆ Stop and read historical roadside markers.

123 ◆ Learn to listen.
Opportunity sometimes
knocks very softly.

124 ◆ Know how to change a tyre.

125 ◆ Know how to tie a bow tie.

126 ◆ Respect your children's privacy. Knock before entering their rooms.

127 ◆ Wear audacious underwear under the most solemn business attire.

128 ♦ Remember people's names.

129 ♦ When starting out, don't worry about not having enough money. Limited funds are a blessing, not a curse. Nothing encourages creative thinking in quite the same way.

130 ♦ Leave the toilet seat in the down position.

131 ♦ Never ask a barber if you need a haircut.

132 ♦ Visit London, and do the tourist bit.

133 ♦ When someone is relating an important event that's happened to them, don't try to top them with a story of your own. Let them have the stage.

134 ◆ Don't buy cheap tools.

135 ◆ Have crooked teeth straightened.

136 ◆ Have dull-coloured teeth whitened.

137 ◆ Keep your watch five minutes fast.

138 ◆ Learn a foreign language.

139 ◆ Never deprive someone of hope; it might be all they have.

140 ◆ Introduce yourself to the manager where you bank. It's important that he/she knows you personally.

141 ◆ Give yourself an hour to cool off before responding to someone who has provoked you. If it involves something really important, give yourself 24 hours.

142 ◆ Pay your bills on time.

143 ◆ Join a softball team.

144 ◆ Take someone bowling.

145 ◆ Keep a torch and extra batteries under the bed and in the glove compartment of your car.

146 ♦ When playing games with children, let them win.

147 ♦ Turn off the television at dinner time.

148 ♦ Learn to handle a pistol and rifle safely.

149 ♦ Skip one meal a week and give what you would have spent to a homeless person.

150 ◆ Sing in a choir.

151 ◆ Get acquainted with a good lawyer, accountant and plumber.

152 ◆ When walking through a room, do one thing to make it more organized and beautiful.

153 ◆ Take time to smell the roses.

154 ◆ Resist the temptation to put a cute message on your answer machine.

155 ◆ Make a will and tell your next-of-kin where it is.

156 ◆ Strive for excellence, not perfection.

157 ◆ Stand up when singing the national anthem.

158 ◆ Pray not for things, but for wisdom and courage.

159 ◆ Be tough-minded but tenderhearted.

160 ◆ Use seat belts.

161 ◆ Have regular medical and dental checkups.

162 ◆ Keep your desk and work area neat.

163 ◆ Take an overnight train trip and sleep in a Pullman.

164 ◆ Be punctual and insist on it in others.

165 ◆ Don't waste time responding to your critics.

166 ♦ Avoid negative people.

167 ♦ Don't scrimp in order to leave money to your children.

168 ♦ Resist telling people how something should be done. Instead, tell them *what* needs to be done. They will often surprise you with creative solutions.

169 ◆ Be original.

170 ◆ Be neat.

171 ◆ Never give up on what you really want to do. The person with big dreams is more powerful than one with all the facts.

172 ◆ Be suspicious of all politicians.

173 ◆ Be kinder
than necessary.

174 ♦ Encourage your children to have a part-time job after the age of sixteen.

175 ♦ Give people a second chance, but not a third.

176 ♦ Read carefully anything that requires a signature. Remember the big print giveth, the small print taketh away.

177 ◆ Never take action when you're angry.

178 ◆ Learn to recognize the inconsequential, then ignore it.

179 ◆ Be your spouse's best friend.

180 ◆ Do battle against prejudice and discrimination wherever you find it.

181 ◆ Wear out, don't rust out.

182 ◆ Be romantic.

183 ◆ Let people know what you stand for –
and what you won't stand for.

184 ◆ Don't quit a job until you've lined up
another.

185 ◆ Never criticize the person who signs your paycheque. If you are unhappy with your job, resign.

186 ◆ Be insatiably curious. Ask 'why' a lot.

187 ◆ Measure people by the size of their hearts, not the size of their bank accounts.

188 ◆ Become the most positive and enthusiastic person you know.

189 ◆ Learn how to fix a leaky tap and toilet.

190 ◆ Have good posture. Enter a room with purpose and confidence.

191 ◆ Don't worry that you can't give your kids the best of everything. Give them *your* very best.

192 ◆ Drink low fat milk.

193 ◆ Use less salt.

194 ◆ Eat less red meat.

195 ◆ Determine the quality of a neighbourhood by the manners of the people living there.

196 ◆ Surprise a new neighbour with one of your favourite homemade dishes – and include the recipe.

197 ◆ Don't forget, a person's greatest emotional need is to feel appreciated.

198 ◆ Feed a stranger's expired parking meter.

199 ◆ Don't carry a grudge.

200 ◆ Park at the back of the car park at shopping centres. The walk is good exercise.

201 ◆ Don't watch violent television shows, and don't buy the products that sponsor them.

202 ◆ Show respect for all living things.

203 ◆ Return borrowed vehicles with the petrol tank full.

204 ◆ Give your best to your employer. It's one of the best investments you can make.

205 ◆ Loosen up. Relax. Except for rare life-and-death matters, nothing is as important as it first seems.

206 ◆ Choose work that is in harmony with your values.

207 ◆ Don't eat just before giving a speech.

208 ◆ Remember that 80 per cent of the success in any job is based on your ability to deal with people.

209 ◆ Observe the speed limit.

210 ◆ Commit yourself
to constant
self-improvement.

211 ◆ Take your dog to obedience school. You'll both learn a lot.

212 ◆ Don't allow the phone to interrupt important moments. It's there for your convenience, not the caller's.

213 ◆ Don't waste time grieving over past mistakes. Learn from them and then move on.

214 ♦ When complimented, a sincere
'thank you' is the only response
required.

215 ♦ Be a good loser.

216 ♦ Be a good winner.

217 ♦ Don't discuss business in lifts. You
never know who may overhear you.

218 ◆ Don't plan a long evening on a blind date. A lunch date is perfect. If things don't work out, both of you have only wasted an hour.

219 ◆ Never go food shopping when you're hungry. You'll buy too much.

220 ◆ Spend less time worrying *who's* right, and more time deciding *what's* right.

221 ♦ Don't major
in minor things.

222 ◆ Think twice before burdening a friend with a secret.

223 ◆ Praise in public.

224 ◆ Criticize in private.

225 ◆ Never tell anyone they look tired or depressed.

226 ◆ When someone hugs you, let them be the first to let go.

227 ◆ Resist giving advice concerning marriage, finances or hair styles.

228 ◆ Have impeccable manners.

229 ◆ Never pay for work before it's completed.

230 ♦ Keep good company.

231 ♦ Keep a daily journal.

232 ♦ Keep your promises.

233 ♦ Avoid any church that has cushions on the pews and is considering building a gymnasium.

234 ◆ Teach your children the value of money and the importance of saving.

235 ◆ Be willing to lose a battle in order to win the war.

236 ◆ Don't be deceived by first impressions.

237 ◆ Seek out the good in people.

238 ◆ Don't encourage rude or inattentive service by tipping the standard amount.

239 ◆ Watch the film *It's A Wonderful Life* every Christmas.

240 ◆ Drink eight glasses of water every day.

241 ◆ Respect tradition.

242 ◆ Be cautious about lending money to friends. You might lose both.

243 ◆ Never waste an opportunity to tell good employees how much they mean to the company.

244 ◆ Buy a bird feeder and hang it so that you can see it from your kitchen window.

245 ◆ Never cut what
can be untied.

246 ♦ Wave at children on school buses.

247 ♦ Tape record your parents' memories of how they met and their first years of marriage.

248 ♦ Show respect for others' time. Call whenever you're going to be more than ten minutes late for an appointment.

249 ◆ Hire people smarter than you.

250 ◆ Learn to show cheerfulness, even when you don't feel like it.

251 ◆ Learn to show enthusiasm, even when you don't feel like it.

252 ◆ Take good care of those you love.

253 ♦ Be modest. A lot was accomplished before you were born.

254 ♦ Keep it simple.

255 ♦ Purchase petrol from your local garage even if it costs more. Next winter when it's six degrees and your car won't start you'll be glad they know you.

256 ◆ Don't jaywalk.

257 ◆ Never ask a lawyer or accountant for business advice. They are trained to find problems, not solutions.

258 ◆ When meeting someone for the first time, resist asking what they do for a living. Enjoy their company without attaching any labels.

259 ◆ Avoid like the plague any lawsuit.

260 ◆ Every day show your family how much you love them with your words, with your touch, and with your thoughtfulness.

261 ◆ Take family holidays whether you can afford them or not. The memories will be priceless.

262 ♦ Don't gossip.

263 ♦ Don't discuss salaries.

264 ♦ Don't nag.

265 ♦ Don't gamble.

266 ♦ Beware of the person who has nothing to lose.

267 ◆ Lie on your back and look up at the stars.

268 ◆ Don't leave car keys in the ignition.

269 ◆ Don't whine.

270 ◆ Arrive at work early and stay beyond quitting time.

271 ◆ When facing a difficult task, act as though it is impossible to fail. If you're going after Moby Dick, take along the tartar sauce.

272 ◆ Change air conditioner filters every three months.

273 ◆ Remember that overnight success usually takes about fifteen years.

274 ♦ Leave everything
a little better
than you found it.

275 ◆ Cut out complimentary newspaper articles about people you know and send the articles to them with notes of congratulations.

276 ◆ Patronize local shops even if it costs a bit more.

277 ◆ Fill your fuel tank when it falls below one-quarter full.

278 ♦ Don't expect money to bring you happiness.

279 ♦ Never snap your fingers to get someone's attention. It's rude.

280 ♦ No matter how dire the situation, keep your cool.

281 ♦ When paying cash, ask for a discount.

282 ◆ Find a good tailor.

283 ◆ Don't use a toothpick in public.

284 ◆ Never underestimate your power to change yourself.

285 ◆ Never overestimate your power to change others.

286 ◆ Practise empathy. Try to see things from other people's points of view.

287 ◆ Promise big. Deliver big.

288 ◆ Discipline yourself to save money. It's essential to success.

289 ◆ Get and stay in shape.

290 ◆ Find some other way of proving your manhood than by shooting defenceless animals and birds.

291 ◆ Remember the deal's not done until the cheque has cleared.

292 ◆ Don't burn bridges. You'll be surprised how many times you have to cross the same river.

293 ◆ Don't spread yourself too thin. Learn to say *no* politely and quickly.

294 ◆ Keep overheads low.

295 ◆ Keep expectations high.

296 ◆ Accept pain and disappointment as part of life.

297 ♦ Remember that a successful marriage depends on two things: (1) finding the right person and (2) being the right person.

298 ♦ See problems as opportunities for growth and self-mastery.

299 ♦ Don't believe people when they ask you to be honest with them.

300 ◆ Don't expect life to be fair.

301 ◆ Become an expert in time management.

302 ◆ Lock your car even if it's parked in your own driveway.

303 ◆ Never go to bed with dirty dishes in the sink.

304 ◆ Judge your success
by the degree that
you're enjoying peace,
health and love.

305 ◆ Learn to handle a handsaw and a hammer.

306 ◆ Take a nap on Sunday afternoons.

307 ◆ Compliment the meal when you're a guest in someone's home.

308 ◆ Make the bed when you're an overnight visitor in someone's home.

309 ♦ Contribute five per cent of your income to charity.

310 ♦ Don't leave a ring round the bath.

311 ♦ Don't waste time playing cards.

312 ♦ When tempted to criticize your parents, spouse or children, bite your tongue.

313 ◆ Never underestimate the power of love.

314 ◆ Never underestimate the power of forgiveness.

315 ◆ Don't bore people with your problems. When someone asks you how you feel, say, 'Terrific.' When they ask, 'How's Business?' reply, 'Excellent.'

316 ◆ Learn to disagree without being disagreeable.

317 ◆ Be tactful. Never alienate anyone on purpose.

318 ◆ Hear both sides before judging.

319 ◆ Refrain from envy. It's the source of much unhappiness.

320 ♦ Be courteous to everyone.

321 ♦ Wave to lollipop ladies.

322 ♦ Don't say you don't have enough time. You have the same number of hours per day as Helen Keller, Pasteur, Michelangelo, Mother Theresa, Leonardo da Vinci, Thomas Jefferson and Albert Einstein.

323 ◆ When there's no time for a full work-out do push-ups.

324 ◆ Don't delay acting on a good idea. Chances are someone else has just thought of it, too. Success comes to the one who acts first.

325 ◆ Be wary of people who tell you how honest they are.

326 ◆ Remember that winners do what losers don't want to do.

327 ◆ When you arrive at your job in the morning, let the first thing you say brighten everyone's day.

328 ◆ Seek opportunity, not security. A boat in a harbour is safe, but in time its bottom will rot out.

329 ◆ Install smoke detectors in your home.

330 ◆ Rekindle old friendships.

331 ◆ When travelling, put a card in your wallet, with your name, home phone number, the number of a friend or close relative, important medical information, plus the phone number of the hotel where you're staying.

332 ◆ Live your life as an
exclamation, not an
explanation.

333 ◆ Instead of using the words *if only*, try substituting the words *next time*.

334 ◆ Instead of using the word *problem*, try substituting the word *opportunity*.

335 ◆ Every so often push your luck.

336 ◆ Get your next pet from the animal shelter.

337 ◆ Reread your favourite book.

338 ◆ Live your life so that your epitaph could read, 'No regrets.'

339 ◆ Never walk out on a quarrel with your partner.

340 ◆ Don't think a higher price always means higher quality.

341 ◆ Don't be fooled. If something sounds too good to be true, it probably is.

342 ◆ When renting a car for a couple of days, splash out on a posh one.

343 ◆ Be bold and courageous. When you look back on life, you'll regret the things you didn't do more than the ones you did.

344 ◆ When someone has rendered a service for you and doesn't know how much to charge, ask, 'What do you think is fair?'

345 ◆ Learn how to operate a computer.

346 ◆ Regarding furniture and clothes: if you think you'll be using them five years or longer, buy the best you can afford.

347 ◆ Never waste an opportunity to tell someone you love them.

348 ◆ Own a good dictionary.

349 ◆ Own a good thesaurus.

350 ◆ Remember the three most important things when buying a home: location, location, location.

351 ◆ Keep valuable papers in a bank safety deposit.

352 ♦ Get organized. Know where you are needed. But if something wonderful and unexpected comes along, be flexible enough to follow it.

353 ♦ Go through all your old photographs. Select ten and tape them to your kitchen cabinets. Change them every month.

354 ◆ To explain a romantic break-up, simply say, 'It was all my fault.'

355 ◆ Evaluate yourself by your own standards, not someone else's.

356 ◆ Be there when people need you.

357 ◆ Let your local Member of Parliament know how you feel.

358 ♦ Be decisive even if it means you'll sometimes be wrong.

359 ♦ Don't let anyone talk you out of pursuing what you know to be a great idea.

360 ♦ Be prepared to lose once in a while.

361 ♦ Never eat the last piece of cake.

362 ♦ Know when to keep silent.

363 ♦ Know when to speak up.

364 ♦ Every day look for some small way to improve your marriage.

365 ♦ Every day look for some small way to improve the way you do your job.

366 ♦ Don't flush public toilets with your hand – use your elbow.

367 ♦ Acquire things the old-fashioned way: save for them and pay cash.

368 ♦ Remember no one makes it alone. Have a grateful heart and be quick to acknowledge those who help you.

369 ◆ Remember the ABC's of success:
ability, breaks, courage.

370 ◆ Do business with those who do
business with you.

371 ◆ Work hard to create in your children
a good self-image. It's the most
important thing you can do to insure
their success.

372 ◆ Give clients your enthusiastic best.

373 ◆ Let your children overhear you saying complimentary things about them to other adults.

374 ◆ Just to see how it feels, for the next 24 hours refrain from criticizing anybody or anything.

375 ◆ Take charge of your attitude. Don't let someone else choose it for you.

376 ◆ Save an evening a week for just you and your partner.

377 ◆ Carry jump leads in your car.

378 ◆ Get all repair estimates in writing.

379 ◆ Forget committees. New, noble, world-changing ideas always come from one person working alone.

380 ◆ Pay attention to details.

381 ◆ Be a self-starter.

382 ◆ Be loyal.

383 ◆ Understand that happiness is not based on possessions, power, or prestige, but on relationships with people you love and respect.

384 ◆ Never give a loved one a gift that suggests they need improvement.

385 ◆ Compliment even small improvements.

386 ◆ Turn off the tap each time you brush your teeth.

387 ◆ Wear expensive shoes, belts and ties, but buy them in a sale.

388 ♦ When undecided about what colour to paint a room, choose antique white.

389 ♦ Carry stamps in your wallet. You never know when you'll discover the perfect card for a friend or loved one.

390 ♦ Street musicians are a treasure. Stop for a moment and listen; then leave a small donation.

391 ◆ Support equal pay for equal work.

392 ◆ Pay your fair share.

393 ◆ Try everything offered by supermarket food demonstrators.

394 ◆ When faced with a serious health problem, get at least three medical opinions.

395 ◆ Remain open, flexible, curious.

396 ◆ Never give anyone a fruitcake.

397 ◆ Never acquire just one kitten. Two are a lot more fun and no more trouble.

398 ◆ Start meetings on time regardless of who's missing.

399 ◆ Focus on making things better, not bigger.

400 ◆ Stay out of nightclubs.

401 ◆ Don't ever watch hot dogs or sausages being made.

402 ◆ Begin each day with some of your favourite music.

403 ◆ Visit your local Crown Court during a trial.

404 ◆ When attending meetings, find a seat at the front.

405 ◆ Don't be intimidated by doctors and nurses. When you're in the hospital, it's still your body.

406 ◆ Visit friends and relatives when they are in hospital; you need only stay a few minutes.

407 ◆ Once in a while, take the scenic route.

408 ◆ Don't let your possessions possess you.

409 ◆ Wage war against litter.

410 ◆ Send a lot of Valentine cards. Sign them, 'Someone who thinks you're terrific.'

411 ◆ Cut your own firewood.

412 ◆ When you and your partner have a disagreement, regardless of who's wrong, apologize. Say 'I'm sorry I upset you. Would you forgive me?' These are healing magical words.

413 ◆ Don't flaunt your success, but don't apologize for it either.

414 ◆ After experiencing inferior service, food or products, bring it to the attention of the person in charge. Good managers will appreciate knowing.

415 ◆ Be enthusiastic about the success of others.

416 ◆ Share the credit.

417 ♦ Read to your children.

418 ♦ Sing to your children.

419 ♦ Listen to your children.

420 ♦ Get your priorities straight. No one ever said on his death bed, 'If I'd only spent more time at the office.'

421 ◆ Take care of your reputation. It's your most valuable asset.

422 ◆ Turn on your headlights when it begins to rain.

423 ◆ Don't drive on someone's tail.

424 ◆ Sign and carry your organ donor card.

425 ◆ Don't allow self-pity. The moment this emotion strikes, do something nice for someone less fortunate than you.

426 ◆ Don't procrastinate. Do what needs doing when it needs to be done.

427 ◆ Don't accept 'good enough' as good enough.

428 ◆ Do more than is expected.

429 ◆ When you know you need help, don't delay in asking for it.

430 ♦ Select a doctor your own age so that you can grow old together.

431 ♦ Use soda water as an emergency spot remover.

432 ♦ Improve your performance by improving your attitude.

433 ♦ Have a friend who owns a van.

434 ◆ Be especially courteous and patient
with older people.

435 ◆ Make a list of 25 things you want to
experience before you die. Carry it in
your wallet and refer to it often.

436 ◆ Have some knowledge of three
religions other than your own.

437 ◆ Answer the phone with enthusiasm and energy in your voice.

438 ◆ Every person that you meet knows something you don't; learn from them.

439 ◆ Tape record your parents' laughter.

440 ◆ Buy cars that have air bags.

441 ◆ When meeting someone you don't know well, extend your hand and give them your name. Never assume they remember you even if you've met them before.

442 ◆ Do it right the first time.

443 ◆ Laugh a lot. A good sense of humour cures almost all of life's ills.

444 ◆ Never underestimate the power of a kind word or deed.

445 ◆ Don't undertip the waiter just because the food is bad; he didn't cook it.

446 ◆ Change your car's oil and filter every three thousand miles regardless of what the owner's manual recommends.

447 ◆ Conduct family fire drills. Be sure everyone knows what to do in case the house catches fire.

448 ◆ Don't be afraid to say, 'I don't know.'

449 ◆ Don't be afraid to say, 'I made a mistake.'

450 ◆ Don't be afraid to say, 'I need help.'

451 ◆ Don't be afraid to say, 'I'm sorry.'

452 ◆ Never compromise your integrity.

453 ◆ Keep a note pad and pencil on your bedside table. Million-dollar ideas sometimes strike at 3 a.m.

454 ◆ Show respect for everyone who works for a living, regardless of how trivial their job.

455 ◆ Read a quality Sunday newspaper to keep informed.

456 ◆ Send your loved one flowers. Think of a reason later.

457 ◆ Attend your children's sports days and recitals.

458 ◆ When you find a job that's ideal, take it regardless of the pay. If you've got what it takes, your salary will soon reflect your value to the company.

459 ◆ Don't use time
or words carelessly.
Neither can be
retrieved.

460 ♦ Look for opportunities to make people feel important.

461 ♦ Reduce your use of cups, plates and containers made of styrofoam.

462 ♦ When a child falls and grazes a knee or elbow, show concern; then take the time to 'kiss it and make it better'.

463 ◆ Be open to new ideas.

464 ◆ Don't miss the magic of the moment by focusing on what's to come.

465 ◆ When talking to the press, remember they always have the last word.

466 ◆ Set short-term and long-term goals.

467 ♦ When planning a trip abroad, read about the places you'll visit before you go or, better still, rent a travel video.

468 ♦ Don't steal other people's thunder.

469 ♦ Stand up when greeting a visitor to your office.

470 ♦ Don't interrupt.

471 ♦ Before leaving to meet a flight, call the airline first to be sure it's on time.

472 ♦ Be more concerned with living wide than living long.

473 ♦ Don't be rushed into making an important decision. People will understand if you need more time.

474 ◆ Be prepared. You never get a second chance to make a good first impression.

475 ◆ Don't expect others to listen to your advice and ignore your example.

476 ◆ Go the distance. When you accept a task, finish it.

477 ◆ Give thanks before every meal.

478 ◆ Don't insist on running someone else's life.

479 ◆ Respond promptly to R.S.V.P. invitations. If there's a phone number, call; if not, write a note.

480 ◆ Take a kid to the zoo.

481 ◆ Watch for big problems.
They disguise big
opportunities.

482 ◆ Get into the habit of putting your car keys in the same place when entering your home.

483 ◆ Learn a card trick.

484 ◆ Steer clear of restaurants that rotate.

485 ◆ Never admit at work that you're tired, angry or bored.

486 ◆ Give people the benefit of the doubt.

487 ◆ Decide to get up half an hour earlier
in the morning. Do this for a year,
and you will add seven and a half
days to your waking world.

488 ◆ Keep an extra key hidden on your car
in case you lock yourself out.

489 ◆ Don't make the same mistake twice.

490 ◆ Don't drive on worn tyres.

491 ◆ Make someone's day by paying the toll for the person in the car behind you.

492 ◆ Put an insulation blanket around your hot water heater to conserve energy.

493 ◆ Save 10 per cent of what you earn.

494 ◆ Never discuss money with people who have much more or much less than you.

495 ◆ Never buy a beige car.

496 ◆ Never buy something you don't need just because it's in a sale.

497 ◆ Don't be called out on strike. Go down swinging.

498 ◆ Question your goals by asking, 'Will this help me become my very best?'

499 ◆ Cherish your children for what they are, not for what you'd like them to be.'

500 ◆ When negotiating your salary, think of what you want; then ask for 10 per cent more.

501 ◆ Keep several irons in the fire.

502 ◆ After you've worked hard to get what you want, take the time to enjoy it.

503 ◆ Be a leader: Remember the one in front is the only one with a decent forward view.

504 ◆ Commit yourself to quality.

505 ◆ Be alert for opportunities to show praise and appreciation.

506 ◆ Never underestimate the power of words to heal and reconcile relationships.

507 ◆ Your mind can only hold one thought at a time. Make it a positive and constructive one.

508 ◆ Become someone's hero.

509 ◆ Marry only for love.

510 ◆ Count your blessings.

511 ◆ Call your mother.